Holy Ghost Hoodoo

The Wonder Working Power of Christian Folk Magic

Darrin W. Owens

© 2017 Darrin W. Owens

All rights reserved. No part of this book may be reproduced or transmitted in any form or by any means whatsoever without express written permission from the author, except in the case of brief quotations embodied in critical articles and reviews. Please refer all pertinent questions to the publisher.

www.psychicdarrinowens.com

Topic Listing

Dedication 4
Author's Note 5
Wilderness Mentality 6
What is Christian Folk Magic? 8
My Folk Magic Heritage 9
The Power of Conjure 14
Moses: The Original Conjure Doctor 16
The Spiritual Forces Within You 18
The Holy Ghost 19
Holy Ghost Hoodoo Essentials 23
What Exactly is the Word of God? 26
Psalmic Prayers 29
Petitions: Prayer Work in Holy Ghost Hoodoo 33
Helpful Spirits of Christian Folk Magic 36
Spiritual Discernment in Folk Magic 51
A Conjurer's Tool Box 55
Altar Work 59
Conjure Herbs, Roots & Curios 69
Holy Ghost Hoodoo Herb Magic: Waking up the Roots 73
Conjure Workings & Formulas 114
Hoodoo, Conjure and Folk Magic Definitions 118
Closing Remarks 123
Bio 124

Dedication:

My contribution to the work of Christian Folk Magic is dedicated to my Great-Grandfather James Lauther Chadwick. I will forever be in debt to his spirit for passing on his blessings to me. His power lives on.

Authors Note:

First and foremost dear reader I have not written this book to proclaim myself a supreme authority on the practice of American folk magic. I have been a clairvoyant, Christian spiritualist minister and published author for over 20 years, and this work is yet another reflection of my exciting journey. The pages you are about to read contain both traditional folk magic teachings, superstitions and my own contemporary adaptations. This work is purely a personal research project born of my own Arkansas Ozark roots. You will find that I use the word Hoodoo in the title. Usually a term associated with African American Folk Magic "Hoodoo" has become a blanket term for many practices of folk magic in the U.S. Let me say here that I have a great respect for Hoodoo (African American Folk Magic) and I have adopted many of its wisdom practices for my own work and give credit to its important part in the world of spiritual healing. In this particular work I will use terms such as Power Doctor, Goomering/Goomer Doctor, Conjure and Rootwork to identify Christian Folk Magic, its practice and the folks who perform it.

Wilderness Mentality

Some things that folks call superstitious is just as true as God's own gospel! - Vance Randolph

In the Bible there is a story about the Israelites who wandered around in the wilderness for forty years to make what was actually an eleven-day journey. The Israelites would not move on because they had a wilderness mentality (wrong mindsets). The Israelites had no positive outlook for their lives, and they lacked the acceptance of God's inherent power to move them in the right direction. Many of us do this very same thing. We keep going around and around the same deserts in our life and instead of making any progress, it takes us many years to realize our spiritual power to overcome all the mountains and valleys in life. Christian Folk Magic can offer us a new mindset. We need to start believing that God's power is available to us. This "Holy Ghost Hoodoo" lives within us and all around us. Matthew 19:26 tells us *that with God all things are possible.*

Everybody wants a better life, but nobody wants to work for it. We take workshops, we meditate and we pray for abundance, love and success, but when it does not show up the blame is laid on karma, or the will of God or even the devil. Sometimes an outside force is the case for challenges, but it's the drive and purpose within us that overcomes obstacles, self-induced or not. Some folks tend to hop to the next bandwagon in hopes of achieving their desires. The foundation of any spiritual practice is this; you have to work at it and with it. You have to know your intentions, and your desires and most of all you have to know how to direct your power to make it happen, without fear. It's time to get out of our wilderness mentality, reshape our thoughts and think with the mind of God, the mind of Creation itself.

If ol' Moses would have shared his "power secrets" with everyone else, perhaps we would not have taken so long to find our way to paradise and out of the wilderness. We all have the potential to manifest "burning bush" moments; we just have to start believing we deserve to work with God's Spiritual Forces just like the prophets and saints of old.

What is Christian Folk Magic?

Christian folk magic is a biblical spiritual practice that developed from a number of folklore traditions in and around the American south passed down through generations. It's based on the act of focused prayerful intentions that change one's life by using one's own personal connection to God's Power.

I suppose it was inevitable that at some point in my metaphysical career as a spiritual author, I would write a book about folk magic. My mother named me "Darrin" after the TV show Bewitched, so from the very beginning there was a sense of the magical initiated into my life. I have been teaching and writing books on intuition and the supernatural for over 20 years. The awakening of folk magic in my life is yet another part of my spiritual journey. Folk magic brought me home like the prodigal son to my roots, where the answers have always been. My spiritual work first began in the mid 90's when my mentor at the time was schooling me in exorcisms and remedying supernatural challenges. When most baby clairvoyants were learning to read auras, and flip through tarot cards, I was discerning spirits and learning how to spot a demon infestation.

The supernatural had always been an open door in my life. I can't remember a time when there was not some sort of ghost or spiritual energy hovering around me. This kind of life was never scary or "out of sorts" to me. There was always a strange normalcy to it. Honestly, I'd be more nervous not seeing moving shadows in the corner of a room.

You will discover, especially in this book, spirits and otherworldly entities have the ability to affect the living, either for healing intentions or for evil; more on that later.

My Folk Magic Heritage

But the Holy Ghost, whom the Father will send in my name, he shall teach you all things, and bring all things to your remembrance, whatsoever I have said unto you. - John 14:26

I grew up in the Ozark Mountains of Arkansas. This is a rugged land filled with country folklore, old-time music and that old-time religion. Most of my great-uncles were preacher men, and they painted on the face of riotousness complete with bible thumping and hell fire.

My mother, my aunt and my grandmother were a bit different. They were God loving Christians, but they had a mystical side to them with an open mind to the otherworldly. My grandma could weave a ghost story that even Stephen King could not top. I remember as a kid staying over at my grandparents' house in the Arkansas Ozark Mountains, trying to go to sleep after being told one of grandma's tales of terror about the axed murdered man with a split head who haunted the old Staggs place down the road. I have to thank my grandma for preparing me for my supernatural future, in her dark comical way. In my ancestral background, Christian Folk Magic practices are born from an Ozark/Appalachian/Native American tradition and reaches further back into European folk beliefs. I have found that the world of Christian Folk Magic is a mixed bag full of lore and historical significance. With this particular research work I lovingly call, Holy Ghost Hoodoo, I'm keeping my roots in the "old time tradition" which is essential to the memory of my ancestors.

From my own personal experiences with countless "workers of the root" everyone has their own flavor of folk magic.

One very interesting perspective on southern style folk magic in general is its influence in protestant Christianity. Although folk magic is not a religion, practitioners were Christian. For decades folks either in the Deep South or high in the Ozark or Appalachian mountain regions used the Holy Bible as a religious document and as a book of powerful prayers and conjuration. People back then did not struggle with the meaning of life like we do today. The old folks "back home" woke up, prayed for their families, the land and the future. They were thankful people, and simple in the fact that the home and hearth were the priorities. Blessings were invoked as much as possible to keep the family and community strong. There was a social nature that brought people together, sharing stories of how the local healer man or granny witch cured their problems with love or health by herb, root and prayer.

I will say here that if you are not believer in the Bible or in Jesus Christ, this work is not for you. There are some folks out there that say you don't have to believe in the Bible or Jesus to do this work. I respectfully disagree. If you don't believe in the Holy Ghost power behind this practice, then why would it work for you?

Keeping Christian Folk Magic traditionally Bible based is how its purity and power keeps flowing. I'm not asking you to convert to being a Christian, just respect and be open minded the power we are talking about here. This work has always been steeped in the Holy Bible, and to water it down would be a disgrace. As a believer, you are under the anointing of Christ, protected and covered by the Holy Ghost in your conjure workings.

In the backwoods of the Ozarks you would never really hear the word "magic." The words often used as far as performing folk magic were fixin', prayin', conjure or doing the "workings." The old terms used for a folk magic practitioner in the Ozarks were Power Doctor or Goomer Doctor. The Power Doctors were mountain healers using the conjure power of verbal incantations like Bible verses and prayer rituals. Goomer Doctor are often terms used interchangeably ("goomer" refers to the removal of witchcraft or "goomering" from a patient) for the same sort of healer. The Power Doctor could also be called the Faith Healer, or Faith Doctor.

Working with the Bible was very common in the South and it has been often considered the most powerful conjure book in existence.

My great grandfather James Lauther Chadwick (1885-1965) was an Arkansas power doctor (healer) with a strong Bible foundation and Cherokee relations. James Lauther's specialty was using Bible verses for healings and blood stopping. Blood stopping, conjured by a Bible verse or a charm, is an inherited gift passed down through a long line of folk magic practitioners. A gesture with the hand, some prayerful phrases, and air blown from the mouth of the healer, create this miraculous practice. After discovering this fascinating family heritage, it answered so many questions about my own spiritual gifts and brought the revelation that I was not the only black sheep in the family. After James Lauther died, a few of his children became staunch Baptist preachers, and the fundamentalism spread like a poison eventually down the line making my childhood less than perfect.

My mother always said that her grandfather was to pass down his "secrets" but never did. I believe that he probably thought there was nobody worthy to pass his "blessings" along to. I feel perhaps I can now do him justice by opening to my own folk magic heritage; a gift from my great-grandfather and all my relations.

To this day my great uncles won't speak of their father's bible magic. They call it silly superstations, even though they saw the wonder working power that came from James Lauther.

The Power of Conjure

But the Holy Ghost, whom the Father will send in my name, he shall teach you all things, and bring all things to your remembrance, whatsoever I have said unto you. - John 14:26

Conjure is 100% pure Holy Ghost Power being drawn forth (invoked, prayed for) through folk magic to effect and produce results. When you pray for a healing or blessing, you are in fact "conjuring" God's power. The word "conjure" gets a bad rap due to years of the superstitious fear of it being associated with witchcraft or black magic.

This is an age old prejudice that I hope to distinguish. If we used the word, "praying" here I'm sure there would be less superstation. But, I have been some folks pray for some pretty nasty things while cloaked under religion. Whether you pray or conjure, it's all in your intent and to me there is not much difference between the two. Conjuring through folk magic focuses on making one's life better through the spiritual power of incantations, not unlike prayer. It focuses on home and hearth, helping oneself and others with everyday living. The main concern for a true Christian folk magic practitioner is the spiritual cleansing and blessing of their homes and keeping their space peaceful; drawing in luck, love and financial security, as well as spiritual protection. Traditionally, the use of the Holy Bible—along with herbs, oils, roots, candles, and curios—make up folk magic. Conjure is not just a practice in a certain type of folk magic, it is a spiritual force and a lifestyle survived though tradition and ancestral knowledge. If you have your intent clear and your prayers coming from a respectful place to help and heal, it will lift you up and give you all you deserve.

I believe that folk magic, or what I loving call *Holy Ghost Hoodoo* is the most powerful and personal connection we can have with the Almighty. The practice brings us into direct union with the Divine and all of the Holy Spirits that abound. Christian folk magic is not in any way a religion, but there is a deep spiritual power to the practice.

Moses: The Original Conjure Doctor

In Christian Folk Magic traditions we look at the prophet Moses as the original Conjure Doctor or Power Doctor. Ordained by the power of the Almighty, he was able to conjure miracles to not only help his people, but also demonstrate the power and realty of God. There have been many heated arguments over conjure and the Christian tradition, many calling it witchcraft. Conjuring through Christian Folk Magic is not witchcraft. Christian Folk Magic calls on the power of the Old Testament, The Psalms, Song of Solomon, The Holy Trinity, Ancestral Spirits, and the Blessed Christian Saints/Prophets. When you add pagan deities into the mix, you are no longer conjuring Christian Folk Magic; you are performing witchcraft. This was the same vein of truth in the days of Moses.

The magicians of the pharaoh were not working with Conjure (The Holy Ghost Power), they were working with witchcraft, and Moses was endowed with Conjure to prove the existence of the Almighty God; and as we know, he did prove it.

Moses represents the true aspect and power of Conjure. A true conjure worker is bestowed by God and the Holy Ghost, and not by any other forms of false gods or the black arts. Even communicating with our spiritual ancestors and such, we do it by the power held within the Holy Trinity and God's Word (The Holy Bible). For fundamentalists to argue that the work of Folk Magic is considered evil would conflict with biblical accounts of God's people using holy water, anointing oils and herbal magic.

As in Moses' time Power Doctors rely on Supernatural forces to carry out their needs and desires. We call on God to work for us, and use the spiritual power in roots, oils and herbs to enhance our own anointing. There is a spirit of Christian Folk Magic that must be re-awakened and returned to its rightful place in the hearts of a practitioner.

Conjuring through Folk Magic was born with the mission and example of Moses. This was the template for the rest of us to rely on for our own work and education. If we can petition Moses to help us hit the re-set button in this work, then we will be blessed with the pure, undiluted power of Holy Ghost Hoodoo.

The Spiritual Forces Within You

This part of the book will focus on the energy of Christian folk magic, and how it works. My many years of training in faith healing prepared me for the understanding of "conjure consciousness" and how we can develop it. Herbs, roots, oils, and candles are instrumental tools in a conjurer's workings, but it's essential to realize that the power doesn't just come from these objects alone, it is your embodiment of God's Spiritual Forces that is the true power manifested. Remember Christian folk magic is blessed by God, amplified by the Holy Ghost. Without connections to the spiritual energy of conjure and it's Biblical foundation, you are simply going through the motions and disrespecting the power of God almighty.

It's not all just magic tricks kiddos, there is a metaphysical science to all of this. If you are a serious student of Christian conjuring, you will want to learn to develop a deeper knowing about your practice.

The Holy Ghost

But ye shall receive power, after that the Holy Ghost is come upon you: and ye shall be witnesses unto the uttermost part of the earth. - Acts 1:8

Let's get to the blessed power of the Holy Ghost in Christian folk magic. Growing up in the South and being raised as a Baptist, the Holy Ghost was often preached about but was never actually explained. Over many years of studying mystical Christianity and other such ancient texts, I began to figure out why there was such a cloak of mystery around the third aspect of the Holy Triad. It represents not so much a mystery but rather a deliberate edict of the liberating force of God's true nature. In my youth, I would hear the discussions of my uncles and cousins—all ministers or deacons—about being blessed by the Holy Ghost or being washed in the salvation of the Holy Ghost.

The only idea I could gather from their "oh so wise teachings" (sarcasm there), was that this Holy Ghost was some sort of ticket out of the fiery depths of hell. Luckily, this is an absurdity. From my own research of the true nature of the Holy Ghost, I found an incredible revelation. The Holy Ghost is the living breath of God. It is the anointer of wisdom, grace, spiritual awakening, and the blessed power of conjure. When this energy is called it helps empower, motivate, protect and deliver your folk magic conjuring with a bang. In the early Christian and Hebrew mystical texts, this divine presence was often referred to as Shekinah or Sophia, the goddess of wisdom. Shekinah is translated as a word for the divine feminine from ancient Hebrew, literally meaning the "dwelling place of God." In sacred temples throughout the early Judeo Christian texts, this divine presence was described as clouds of smoke that manifested during sacred rituals. Moses was communicated with by the "Shekinah" via the burning bush.

So in essence, the Spirit of God connected to mankind and created "dwelling places" for the union of the physical and spiritual being.

In essence the Holy Ghost anoints God's power in your folk magic practice. The reason the Holy Ghost has been viewed as feminine in nature resides in the fact that its essence is that of a comforter, healer, and counselor. Just as a loving mother provides a child with comfort, help, and guidance, so operates the Holy Ghost in your life. But, the Holy Ghost can also act like a mama bear, protecting her cub with justice, vengeance and fear. You can see why power-hungry religions might try to hide her true nature from the masses. If you give power to the people and show them how connected they are to God on their own merit, there might be no need for a religion at all. Personal conjure workings with the Holy Ghost is very liberating. The time has come for the institutions founded by external power and egocentric religious attitudes to step aside, for a true revival of the Holy Ghost is upon us. We are awakening to her spirit-led power because we know she resides within us and is a gift from the Almighty. We can call on her Power at any time.

Now about the spiritual gifts (the special endowments of supernatural energy), brethren, I do not want you to be misinformed.
- I Corinthians 12:1

The Holy Ghost can bestow on a Christian conjure worker many miraculous gifts. The bible tells us that each one of us is *given the manifestation of the [Holy] Ghost [the evidence, the spiritual illumination of the Spirit] for the good and profit. To one is given in and through the [Holy] Spirit [the power to speak] a message of wisdom, and to another [the power to express] a word of knowledge and understanding according to the same [Holy] Ghost; To another [wonder-working] faith by the same [Holy] Ghost, to another the extraordinary powers of healing by the one Spirit; To another the working of miracles, to another prophetic insight (the gift of interpreting the divine will and purpose); to another the ability to discern and distinguish between [the utterances of true] spirits [and false ones], to another various kinds of [unknown] tongues, to another the ability to interpret [such] tongues.* So you can see how important it is to have the Holy Ghost anoint your work. To close, keep in mind that the Holy Ghost is the anointer, the power within your conjure. The Holy Ghost will amplify your clairvoyant abilities, your communication with spirits, you healing abilities and will aid in psychic protection.

Simple Holy Ghost Invocation: *Come Holy Ghost, Anoint Me Now. By The Power of the Holy Trinity, Come to My Aid.*

Holy Ghost Hoodoo Essentials

THE BIBLE: The Holy Bible is the foundation for truth, non-filtered, Christian Folk Magic. I know that a lot of folks have been hurt by Christianity; but remember that churches or run by people! Don't throw the baby out with the bathwater

THE ALTAR: The altar is a sacred space of power for a worker. Whether you are working with your ancestors, doing blessings work, or drawing money, the altar is where all workings are prayers are performed.

PRAYER: Prayer is the act of calling down, conjuring or drawing to you, the power of Gog in your work. Prayer and Petitions opens the door between you and the Holy Ghost, and then a connection is made. From that act of prayer the power of Christian Folk Magic begins

PETITIONS: Petitions are one of the oldest forms of prayer work– they are found in the Holy Bible as well as other holy texts. The word petition indicates the writing down of a prayer or formula that aims at creating a specific desired outcome or blessing.

THE ANCESTORS: In my Holy Ghost Hoodoo Tradition we know that spirits of our ancestors dwell in the supernatural worlds, and they have the power to influence the fate and fortune of the living via God's will. But honoring them, and petitioning their help they empower our work and bless its direction and progress. Respect the dead, and they will respect you in most cases.

The Holy Bible

In traditional mountain folk magic and southern hoodoo many practitioners were protestant Christians. In the Arkansas hills reverends and preacher men were often looked at as spirit-led folks who drew down the power of God in their healing services.

Like my great grand-father he was a spirit-led healer using the Bible to conjure his craft to help others.

The Bible is the word of God so its power is limitless for the anointed believer. Hillfolks of the Ozark and Appalachian roots, and even the Pennsylvania Dutch circles firmly believed in the strength of scriptural prayer and the power of the Bible to cure the spiritual and physical ills of their society. The effectiveness of prayer was also widely used as a mode of blessing in league with the book of Psalms. These Psalmic prayers were recited over candles and oil lamps as granny witches, or power doctors allowed themselves to be possessed by the Holy Ghost to empower their workings. There were also conjurers who used Bible power in connection with roots and herbs. There is an incredible amount of scripture using Biblical herbs for healing, cleanings and protection. For example the hyssop herb is mentioned in Psalm 51 of the Bible as a spiritual purifier, as it states: *Purge me with hyssop and I shall be clean; wash me and I shall be whiter than snow.* Folk magic lore details the spiritual properties brought about by roots, flowers, oils and herbs, but when they are blessed by the power brought about by word of God, their influence is unsurpassed.

What exactly is the Word of God?

In my experience the word of God is not just a particular spiritual teaching. The Word of God is any words of power that you conjure in the names of the Holy Trinity; the Father, Son and Holy Ghost. The Bible proclaims in Psalm 82:6, "We are gods and children of the most high." If that is in fact the case, then we all have the wonder working power of God, and can achieve the ability to create heaven on earth. If we are made in his image, then prayer and the ability to conjure is born into our very souls. When I was a child I remember my favorite part of going to the Baptist church was the singing. Back home there was not a little church in the Ozarks that did not have multiple copies of the Heavenly Highway Hymns book. In order for the preacher man to call down the spirit of God to bless the flock, Gospel music sung from the Heavenly Highway Hymns book. Gospel or God-spell means, good news. Churchgoers would sing gospel music to invoke the good news of the Lord in preparation for Sunday service and raise the Spirit.

Singing and chanting to call God has always been a staple in any religious setting, and in Christian folk magic, it's no different. One of my favorite gospel songs even to this day is, "There is Power in the Blood." I truly believe the author of this old standard tune must have had some conjure awareness because; pleading the Blood of Jesus is an extremely powerful practice in Christian Folk Magic.

There is pow'r, pow'r, wonder-working pow'r, In the blood of the Lamb; There is pow'r, pow'r, wonder-working pow'r, In the precious blood of the Lamb. - Lewis E. Jones 1899

The "Blood of the Lamb" mentioned in the gospel song above is of course in reference to the Blood of Jesus Christ. If you are working scriptural prayers, this is the most powerful conjuration of all. My grandma would often say things like, "oh that poor person they suffer the Wounds of Jesus." or if she was not too happy with someone she'd say, "I ought to plead the Blood of Jesus on em! That will fix em!" I did not know then but grandma had her own ways of conjuring and she sure had a temper!

Pleading the Blood of Jesus is believed to achieve the ultimate reversal of curses, hexes and completely stop the Devil and his minions in their tracks. Here is a simple conjure prayer to plead the Blood of Jesus for protection and to ward off evil.

I plead the Blood of Jesus Christ over my home, my family and myself. The Blood of Jesus protects me. The Blood of Jesus heals me. The Blood of Jesus avenges me. May all my enemies known and unknown be washed in the Blood of the Lamb. I am free from the devils snare through the Wonder Working Power of the Blood. Amen.

There are so many useful prayers in the Bible, and it does not hurt to have a few in your pocket and see which one does the trick. Saying your prayers in the Name of Jesus Christ guarantees active power in the words. Christ is our redeemer and because of his sacrifice we are all invited to be powerful children of God. 'Christ' literally means the Word of God made flesh (the Anointed one).

Psalmic Prayers

There are 150 psalms altogether that cover a gamut of prayer workings from luck, love, healing and abundance, to stamping out enemies and warding off evil doings. There is just too many to list in one chapter, but I'll add a few here to wet your whistle with. The Psalms are among the most commonly used in the traditional practices of Christian folk magic. Psalmic prayers were also deep traditional practice for mountain folks as well. These verses are often prayed, in whole or in part, during the course of performing a blessing or for altar workings. A few of the Psalms and their remedies are including here:

Psalm 3: For relief a headache or backache

Psalm 10: To exorcise an unclean spirit

Psalm 15: For mental peace

Psalm 31: For protection from back-biting, and gossip

Psalm 65: For road opening that breaks through to success

Psalm 76: For the Lord's intercession, to provide protection from all confrontations

Psalm 112: To increase in power, for success and blessings

Psalm 145: To cleanse and purify those who are affected by ghosts

Psalm 150: For the triumph of the Lord and giving thanks for His interventions

Psalms and Bible verses are typically prayed with a focused intent. They may be performed at an altar, over candles, or during spiritual bathing rituals. Psalms can also be written on paper and placed under a candle vigil, carried on your person or a blessing bag. There are some workers that tear pages out of the bible to burn in offering pots, or use the ashes in a healing oil. I personally do not do this. My grandma would have tanned my hide up and down for something like that. A torn bible was looked at as bad luck in my family, but to each his or her own. Follow your intuition. I feel it's best to write down the few phrases from a psalm you like, or jot it down in its entirety in your own hand.

Since I chose to not add every psalm to this chapter, I will discuss the most powerful psalm of the all, Psalm 23. Honestly, along with the "Our Father" Matthew 6:9-13, I use Psalm 23 all the time for just about everything in my personal practice. I have found it covers all bases. Psalm 23 is the most well-known psalm. It is an all-purpose invocation covering all the basics of life; love, prosperity, protection and guidance.

Psalms 23

The LORD is my shepherd; I shall not want. (Prosperity)

He maketh me to lie down in green pastures: he leadeth me beside the still waters. (Guidance)

He restoreth my soul: he leadeth me in the paths of righteousness for his name's sake. (Healing)

Yea, though I walk through the valley of the shadow of death, I will fear no evil: for thou art with me; thy rod and thy staff they comfort me. (Protection & Blessing)

Thou preparest a table before me in the presence of mine enemies: thou anointest my head with oil; my cup runneth over. (Respect)

Surely goodness and mercy shall follow me all the days of my life: and I will dwell in the house of the LORD forever. (Love & Good Luck)

The Lord's Prayer found in Matthew 6:9-13, is traditionally a supreme conjuration for spiritual cleansing in traditional hoodoo and mountain folk magic systems. I recite this at my working altar every morning before sunrise to clear the day, and open the roads to God's blessings.

Our Father which art in heaven, Hallowed be thy name.

Thy kingdom come, Thy will be done in earth, as it is in heaven

Give us this day our daily bread. And forgive us our trespasses, as we forgive those who trespass against us.

And lead us not into temptation, but deliver us from evil

For thine is the kingdom, and the power, and the glory, forever. Amen.

If you are ready to add some Bible conjure into your practice, first of course, you'll need to fetch a Bible. You can also use the Book of Psalms, as a standalone too. Some workers use their old family Bibles; others purchase a brand new one. I prefer the Amplified Bible, but any variety of translations will do.

Petitions: Prayer Work in Holy Ghost Hoodoo

Spiritual petitions are one of the oldest forms of prayer work—they are found in the Holy Bible as well as in other holy texts. The word petition indicates a written prayer or formula that seeks to create a specific, desired outcome or blessing. In the old folk magic belief systems, petitions are essential to the practice. I believe that petition work truly improves your hands-on experience with the Almighty and is much more meaningful than empty prayers of pleading and begging. I have always taught that prayer is a two-way street and must be a practice of merging the Creator with the one who is praying. In the old days, petitions were written on brown paper similar to that of a paper bag.

Paper bags were easily accessible to people who might be poor, lived in the hills, and also practiced Christian Folk Magic and healing work. "Fancy paper," in most cases, was not available or affordable. Nowadays, we know that a petition is a formal, written request appealing to authority—in this case a spiritual authority— with respect to a particular cause or outcome. Petitions generally need to be written on a balanced piece of paper where the sides are equal. It is thought that the balance is what helps direct the energy of the desired outcome.

I personally like to use brown paper in memory of the old practitioners of long ago. A petition is written about what you want to attract, bless, prevent, or protect. Remember that a petition acts as a specific desire to be helped and influenced on your behalf by God. As you write out your petition—through affirmation or request—you are giving specific directions about the help that you want from the spiritual powers. The goal of a petition is to create a change in a situation concerning yourself or someone else. This practice is a wonderful tool for sending a blessing or for ensuring spiritual protection.

When I write out my petitions I always date and sign it. You need to make sure your intent is clear. Date:

Name:

Petition:

Signed_____

When I finish writing out a petition, I like to place it on my altar. The placement of my petition seated on a powerful saint card or under a specific candle helps to empower its spiritual energy. If you are looking for justice in your life, place your petition on your altar with a Saint Michael statue or candle. Petition his fine justice on your behalf. You can write out the petition to Saint Michael and by placing it on your altar dedicated to him—trust me—he will get the message! Pray at your altar every day, not in desperation, but in sweet surrender, and rest assured that you are being cared for. Use the same method for healing. A statue of Jesus or the Archangel Raphael, along with your petition for healing, may be placed on your altar.

This process helps you to have a hands-on experience with your prayer and altar work. It is no longer an empty task of asking for divine help. Instead, you are working an authentic process and literally calling in the Divine by ritual and faithful dedication. One thing to remember is to constantly maintain a clear intention. The Almighty is always watching out for you and has your best interests at heart.

Helpful Spirits of Christian Folk Magic

The power and presence of the dead is very sacred in the work of conjure. American Indian, mountain folk magic, European, African, New Orleans Voodoo, and southern Hoodoo traditions all carry strong connections to the dead as a spiritually protective relationship. Many other religious paths have various ways of honoring and working with the ancestors such as working with the saints and prophets. Catholics petition saints to aid them in their spiritual healing and everyday events and circumstances. Our elders and family members who have passed on can also be empowered to aid us. Even ancestors that may not be a part of our own biological tribe can enter into our and sphere of influence and direct us.

We must remember that the dead were once living and breathing on this earth and are now charged with the sacred task of helping humans on this side of the veil, so a respect nature in this aspect of conjure work should not a question.

The Holy Trinity

The Power of Three is an important conjuration in Christian folk magic. It's usually the invocation at the beginning and ending of prayer work. The number three is frequently used in hoodoo traditions in a variety ways. Most significantly, this reflects the Holy Trinity of the God the Father, God the Son, and God the Holy Ghost. Within the mystical Christian teachings the Holy Trinity, the Father is Yahweh; the Son is Jesus Christ, the Anointed One; and the Holy Ghost is the Shekinah (Divine Wisdom) symbolized in Christianity as a pure white Dove or as White Light.

Prayers said with the Holy Trinity generally conclude with phrases like, In the name of the Father, the Son and Holy Ghost or by the power of three, I conjure thee.

Some folk-magical workers, like me, recite these holy names as the closing words to an incantation while drawing the sign of the cross in the air three times. The invocation of these triple action spirits add power and protection to your conjure; clear and focused.

Holy Trinity Incantation

The power of thee, God the Father, God the Son and God the Holy Ghost, I conjure thee. Bless me by the power of your holy spirit and bring the sacred into all of my workings. I honor your presence and give thanks for your guidance. By the power of three, I conjure thee.

Ancestral Spirits

Ancestral guides are spirits that can assist us in our daily lives. Your ancestral guides are usually family members from previous generations who have become helpers and protectors for future generations. Working with ancestors is a very important part of many cultures. Even in the Ozarks of Arkansas, the dead are important to many of the living. The ancestors' spiritual legacies, their meaning to those who remain behind, and even their intervention for the living are essential in conjure life.

An ancestor is often that of a blood relative. Adoptive ancestors will also give assistance and guidance when called upon. The assistance of the ancestral spirit, La Madama is a good example of this idea of an adoptive ancestor. Ever since I was young, I can remember one ancestral being that has always been around me. Her name is La Madama. Folk legend has it that La Madama is the spirit of an old slave woman who had been a conjure doctor, fortune-teller and spiritual healer. Old-fashioned "Aunt Jemima" pancake mix advertising art or "Mammy" style cookie jar figures are images often used to represent La Madama.

La Madama is often depicted with a broom—a tool symbolic of cleansing away negativity, and sweeping in good fortune. She is also believed to be a guiding force for psychic readers and practioners. She is a "tell it like it is" ancestral archetype, which is perfect for me, since I'm a bit brassy myself.

Prayer to La Madama

Light a candle and set out a cup of strong black coffee, she loves coffee. You can also choose light a pure tobacco cigarette, as you pray the following prayer below. I have found she responds to tobacco offerings very well. If tobacco is not an option, coffee and pure intent will do the trick.

O Holy Spirit of La Madama, I humbly pray. Please give me your sublime intervention for protection, guidance and help.

In the name of the Father, the Son and the Holy Ghost, I ask for your help.

Use your Divine Wisdom and Power of Intercession so that no man nor woman, spell or curse, hex or charm, root, stone or bone, under the eyes of God, may harm me (or name who you are praying for). I ask this with full respect, pure faith and trust in God my Creator and Redeemer. In the name of Him, before who's Glory, Angels shield their faces. Amen.

These spirit helpers can answer your calls, intervene, and petition the Creative Forces on your behalf, if needed. Buy honoring them, and petitioning their help they empower your conjure work and bless its direction and progress.

Ancestral Invocation

I call upon my blood ancestors known and unknown, and all my relations who love and support me. I call upon my ancestral guides who have adopted me as their own. Bless me with your wisdom and insight. Guard and protect me. Let me be a vessel for your spiritual power. By the power of three, I conjure thee! In the name of the Father, the Son and the Holy Ghost. Amen.

Indian Spirit Guides

I often categorize Indian spirit guides under the umbrella of ancestral guides. In my personal conjure work; Indian spirit guides have always carried ancestral energy. There is a deep river of Cherokee blood in my family tree. Indian spirits are truly wise in the ways of the earth, herbal healing, shamanistic ritual, and just pure knowing.

An Indian spirit guide is an important source of conjure in folk magic and southern hoodoo. This leads me to the amazing magic of Black Hawk. Even though Black Hawk lived and died in the Midwestern region of the United States, his spirit has lived and guided many conjure workers in the ways of spiritualism.

Black Hawk was a Native American Sauk and Fox tribe leader who lived from 1767 to 1838. In his lifetime, he earned a reputation as a fierce and cunning warrior who resisted governmental oppression. He also proved to be a wise leader who demonstrated great mercy and insight. Working with the spirit of Black Hawk became very popular in the twentieth century during the spiritualist movement in New Orleans. Spiritual leaders from the upper Midwest who relocated to the South shared the stories and legends of the very powerful Black Hawk, and soon his guidance became rooted and established with great success. Black Hawk is often summoned to help with psychic protection and liberation from oppressors.

In traditional folk ways, healers and conjure doctors who work with the spiritual guidance of Black Hawk customarily place a bucket filled with earth on an altar, upon which stands a statue of a Native American Indian man. Gifts of fruit and tobacco are placed before Black Hawk, and meditation, prayers, and other offerings are made, as well. In my work, Black Hawk is an archetypal force that represents the many faces and powers of an Indian Spirit Guide.

Graveyard Spirits

Graveyard spirits and graveyard conjure are an essential part of folk magic. Although it seems odd that Christian Folk Magic practitioners communicate and work with the dead, it is part of our practice. There is no death, just another state of being. Sometimes the dead will have a more in-depth power and insight to something that we on this side of the realm can't figure out or reach with our own conjure. The connections to the supernatural realms are of extreme importance to deepening your workings, so if you are squeamish about the dead, or have a fear of cemeteries, get yourself over it.

As a Christian conjurer you will at some point be called to be a walker between worlds, and to learn to navigate those realms and discern the spirits and their powers. Just like in life there are nice folks, and not so nice folks. Same goes for the realms of graveyard spirits. You have to know which spirits you can work with, and which spirits keep at arm's length. You want a spirit to help your magic, not rob it.

The friendly-dead are souls that have risen to higher level of consciousness in the spirit realms after death and have chosen to be of helpful service for the living. These of course are your ancestors, and ancestral guides, ministers, healers, doctors and the list can go on. Most often these folks were generally good people while alive.

Then you have the un-friendly dead who are the completely opposite of anything good. These ill-disposed souls chose to stay within the borderlands of the spirit realms and not move higher in consciousness at all. If they were a selfish and malevolent person in body, they are the same out of body and in some cases even worse. Not having a physical body can liberate a spirit, and it can go either way as far as the use of their power in light or dark.

There are some non-believing sorcerers out there that use un-friendly or the intranquil dead for cursing and even love spells. I do not recommend this for the conjure newbie, and as Christian folk magic folks, we don't do that. I don't like to set up rules here, but being an exorcist I have seen many new workers lives fall apart due to working with the unfriendly-dead. A few have come to me for cleansings, and it's a huge ordeal to banish a soul that one has made a pact with. It's dangerous for all involved.

When one feels like they can call on the dead for any service they want, the ego can get in the way, if you are not skilled in years of practice and discernment. This particular book is not intended to go into detail on the hardcore conjure of the graveyard, so I will say this; as a beginning conjurer please work with the spirits you know first. Get comfortable working with ancestors and friendly spirits and then over time if you feel called to perform more graveyard conjure, you can then move deeper into your craft. You want to build of your spiritual protection as well, with the friendly spirits. This is called creating your spiritual court.

Over time you will come to realize the spirits that have chosen to work with your which will most likely be a combination of your ancestral guide, friendly-dead, saints and so on. You can then work on strengthening your relationship with those guides through prayer, communication, meditation and contact with these spirits at your spiritual altars.

Learn as much as you can about your personal spiritual court, including the spirits names, traits offerings, and how best to follow their guidance. These spirits will act as the conduit for divine inspiration, protection and guidance you.

Angels & Saints

In traditional mountain folk magic you would not see a lot of workings with angles or saints. Being mostly protestant Christians, practitioners would conjure the Holy Trinity. Deep in the southern delta regions of the U.S. where the folk magic practices of hoodoo reigned, working with these types of conjure spirits are essential.

I have found it to be a wonderful addition to my own work and as a matter of fact I have been working with the Christian saints and angelic powers since I was a very young psychic reader. Even though I was raised in a rigid Southern Baptist tradition, I developed an affinity for the catholic saints and angels. As in most religions, the honored dead of Christianity's holy men and women known for their spiritual devotions and miracles—are referred to as "saints" or holy persons. The Catholic Church established the concept of the "intercession of saints" many years ago. This idea maintains that saints have a direct connection to God and that prayers made by them in heaven are more powerful or efficacious than prayers made on earth by regular folk. Honestly, all of us have a direct connection to God. Nevertheless, working with the saints and angels and exemplifying their spiritual attributes can, in fact, magnify your folk magic practice beautifully.

Legendary miracles and healings connected to a saint's life made him or her a patron or supporter of certain life situations and conditions here on earth. We can ask for a particular saint's blessing in a multitude of areas in our own lives. Angels, like saints can be called on as well to take you conjure workings to their fullest potential. The archangels seem to be a more popular source of Christian Folk Magic. I'm sure it's due to their high powered ranking in the heavenly realms. Archangels are the closest beings to the Creator, so their power can be limitless to what it can do for your craft. I work with two archangels in Holy Ghost Hoodoo—the Archangel Michael, for justice, cleansings and protection and the Archangel Raphael, for healing and blessing works. One of my dedicated saints that I am honored to be in sync with is Padre Pio. Padre Pio (May 25, 1887 – September 23, 1968) is a highly revered and effective saint for exorcism, protection and healing work. He was a devout Christian mystic who carried the stigmata, the wounds of Christ. He worked miracles, fought with demons and healed many people in his day.

Not unlike working with ancestral spirits and Indian spirits, you go about connecting with these high level beings by intuiting which angel and saint you have always been akin to. Padre Pio is my own patron Saint. Let me say here that the Padre will not work with just anybody. "They must come to the Cross!" he said to me some time ago. If you are a devout Christian, he will work with you. Saints have their own personal devotions to. We must respect that.

A Few Saints and their Folk Magic Associations

MOTHER MARY: Petitioned for compassion, mercy and clearing evil.

ST. ANTHONY: Petitioned to recover lost things.

ST. CLARE: Petitioned for clairvoyance and clarity.

ST. FRANCIS OF ASSISI: Petitioned to protect animals and nature

ST. JOHN THE BAPTIST: Petitioned for baptism, cleanings and purification.

ST. MICHAEL THE ARCHANGEL: Petitioned for protection, exorcism, and justice.

ST. JOAN OF ARC: Petitioned for courage and to overcoming enemies.

ST. MARTHA THE DOMINATOR: Petitioned for justice, money problems and dominating lovers and enemies.

ST. RAPHAEL THE ARCHANGEL: Petitioned for healing and spiritual restoration.

ST. PADRE PIO: Petitioned for exorcism, protection, healing and miracles.

SAINT PETER: Petitioned for open roads, success and block busting.

ST. EXPEDITE: Petitioned for pressings needs, fast luck and quick problem solving.

ST. JOSEPH: Petitioned for employment, real estate, and family blessings.

ST. JUDE: Petitioned for hopeless causes.

HOLY TRINITY: Petitioned to clear evil and draw in blessings, luck, money and success.

Spiritual Discernment in Folk Magic

IMPORTANT: Always test the spirits! Ask the Holy Ghost to empower you with the gift of discernment by reciting this verse and keeping it to heart: *By this you know and recognize the Spirit of God: every spirit that acknowledges and confesses [the fact] that Jesus Christ has [actually] come in the flesh [as a man] is from God [God is its source]- 1 John 4:2*

Discernment is not a word you hear too often in folk magic practices these days. Let me tell you here and now, if you are going to be a TRUE, honest to goodness Christian conjurer, you best get real familiar with discernment on a first name bases. As with any spiritual system it's imperative that you know what you are doing, and most important KNOW the spirits you are working with. The Hierarchy in my *Holy Ghost Hoodoo* practice is the Holy Trinity, my Ancestors and then any other Spirits I choose to work with. There is a reason the Bible states, that one must TEST the spirits. This is one of the essential Gifts of the Holy Ghost. The above comment is a flawless way to keep you and your conjure workings safe and protected.

If you proclaim the Holy Trinity as your foundation, then you will be standing on firm ground. The listings of spirits below are beings that should not be messed with while working with Christian Folk Magic. You may run into these spectral spooks from time to time.

USE CAUTION. It is in your best interest not to associate yourself or your conjure work with these entities. Don't strike a deal, and don't think you can trap them for personal gain. Once you start working with these beings, you're caught in a dangerous web and remember in this case, everyone's bill comes due. There have been conjure workers who have lost their soul to these buggers, so don't be stupid. These nasty spirits love to feed off ignorance, fear, and most of all inflated egos.

Intranquil Spirits: Contrary to popular belief, these spirits are not to be messed with. In some forms of hoodoo these spirits are called on for the most desperate of love spells. There is the ridiculous notion that a conjure worker can bag an intranquil spirit for their bidding. NOT. The intranquil spirit is very close to that of a vengeful spirit except these beings are lost and lonely; a dead soul if you will.

They will torment those that call on them and a worker will pay the price. Don't mess with them. If an intranquil spirit attaches to you they can become extremely jealous of people in your life and hurt the ones you love. Ultimately, they will harm you and in a twisted way and try to keep all your attention and life force directed at them.

Vengeful Spirits: Close to that of the intranquil Spirits, vengeful spirits are all about rage, revenge and harm. To become a vengeful spirit one has died in extreme violence, anger or hatred. A vengeful spirit could have been the victim at their death or even the perpetrator. Some folks were good people when they were alive but at death for whatever reason they turned hateful and became vengeful. Also really rotten folks who die can also stay that way as they take on their own vengeful nature. So in essence, you never know what you're working with. Some non-believing workers are using these spirits for revenge work, and that will always come with a big price that you will not want to pay. There is a vast difference between justice work and revenge work.

Justice work is by the power of the Almighty, and revenge work is conjured by the hand of personal hatred, and when it's attached to a vengeful spirit everyone pays the price. I have seen folks literally lose their souls to a vengeful spirit.

Demons: Hello! Within the Christian Folk Magic tradition there were only two souls on the planet that could control demons, Jesus Christ and King Solomon. You are not one of them! Christian conjurers do not need to be messing with demons.

The only time a worker may cross a demons path is if they conjure one, or when they are trying to exorcise someone from its manipulation and possession. Even then a practitioner may not have the gift of exorcising demons, so it's best to find some help from a minister blessed with true exorcism power. Here is the deal, you mess with demons and you may very well pay the price with your soul, plain and simple.

A Conjurer's Tool Box: Altars, Herbs, Roots, Oils, Candles & Curios

Now we are getting into some fun stuff in the practice of Christian Folk Magic; the conjure tools of the trade. Tools like herbs, roots, oils and the like are the devices of folk magic practioners. In fact, the occult use of such tools in creating spells and rituals is traditional Christian Folk Magic at its finest. Ordinary items like herbs and oils, supplies from the kitchen or farm can function as energetic controls to help direct one's life and wellbeing. These tools are used to help bring about good luck, spiritual blessings, and invoke protection. I must stress that the power of conjure through folk magic comes from your focused and direct intent in league with the Creative Forces of the universe. These tools for which we are about to explore, are extensions of your intention, and their appropriate magical and spiritual properties aid you in the fulfillment of your conjured desire and prayer work.

Some of the tools that we will explore in this chapter will be conjure herbs, roots and flowers. Also discussed will be a variety of curio items such as conjure bags, black hen feathers, broom straws and red brick dust.

HERB/ROOT: Herbs and roots are essential to Christian Folk Magic. Their spiritual properties are the bases for many conjure oils, powders, washes, candles and conjure bags. Working with herbs and roots is the main reason why many folk magic practitioners are known as rootworkers.

OIL: Hoodoo oils, anointing oils and dressing oils have been a permanent fixture in Southern folk magic history, mostly African American hoodoo. Oils are used to carry and enhance the power of conjure ingredients and workings. Many oils such as olive oil, vegetable oil and almond oil are used as the base for a variety of magical formulas in rootwork.

WATER: Water is used in conjure for cleansings, washes, baths, blessings and feeding your ancestral spirits. Herbs and perfumes can also be added to water. Old-time Florida Water stands as a good example. All in all, Water is the magnifier of spirit in your work.

CANDLE: Candle burning has been an ancient art of magic and prayer since the Old Testament days. Candles are used in conjure to draw the spirit of the work, enhance it and empower it. Colored candles are important to the art of hoodoo candle burning.

- White Candles: Purity, spirit and protection
- Red Candles: Passion, love and courage
- Yellow Candles: Good luck, inspiration and power
- Blue Candles: Peacefulness, healing and restoration
- Green Candles: Abundance, money possible and fortune
- Black Candles: Uncrossing, cleanings and jinx removing.
- Pink Candles: Love, friendship and faith.
- Orange Candles: Change, transformation and road opening
- Purple Candles: Spiritual wisdom, mastery and protection
- Brown Candles: Balance and grounding

POWDER: Powders are used for hot foot workings, sachet powders and floor sweeps. Like conjure oils, they enhance your work and draw additional power. Powders are mixed with herbs and other Conjure curios to create desired effects. Graveyard dirt, goofer dust, salt, sugar, red brick dust and sulfur powder also fall under the conjure powder category.

BONE: Bones have been used for divination and luck drawing Christian folk magic for centuries. Bones carry a power, mostly that of a connection between the living and the dead. The mysterious black cat bone, a hoodoo favorite, has been thought to bring good luck, power and success in love and money. The bone of a raccoon penis is also well admired in the conjure world. In Ozark folk magic, this particular bone was made into a lucky charm for love work.

ANIMAL CURIO: Animal parts have been a great source for drawing luck and adding spiritual power to folk magic. Chicken feet for cleansing, alligator claw for luck and money works, the lucky rabbits foot, badger teeth for gamblers luck, and chicken eggs are used to absorb negativity and help in spiritual cleansing work.

Altar Work

For he built altars for all the host of heaven in the two courts of the house of the LORD. - 2 Kings 21:5

Altar work is the name practitioner's use for any kind of spiritual ritual that is performed at an altar to seek the guidance of God, by means of prayer, invocations, chants or Psalmic incantations. Altars can come in a variety of forms, from the lavish and magnificent to small altars on a nightstand or coffee table. People who work with and petition their ancestors, saints, or guides such as Black Hawk may create specialized altars to honor their chosen deity. A conjure altar is traditionally sustain by a long held family customs, magical training, and personal tastes. Creating and maintain altars in Christian Folk Magic, is essential to your personal practice. An altar represents the seat of your power; a physical place where the Holy Ghost can connect with you. It's not only a place where you go for devotional connection and workings; it's also a sacred space where you can recharge your inner resources. I do the majority of my altar works in the early morning. Before the sun rises, I offer prayers to God and my ancestors.

I send blessings to family and friends, to clients and students. As the sun rises the blessings are raised and are sent out to God's Universe to manifest, draw in and increase the desires spoken. I do justice, protection and spiritual cleansing works at sunset to symbolize the removal of negativity, and decreasing that which I do not desire in my life. As the sun goes down, negativity goes with it. At times when I have heavy duty conjure work to do, the darkness of midnight guides my prayers.

Think of it this way, light conjure goes with the rising of the sun and the opening of the horizon, and dark conjure goes with the ascension of the moon and the shadows of night. Light conjure is the drawing in of blessings, good luck and increase workings and dark conjure is best for the drawing out of negativity, bad luck and for performing justice work. I use the term "dark" not in the sense of "evil doings", but in the sense of performing more intensive conjure work "after dark".

I do a lot of my exorcism type work after dark…and into the early morning hours after midnight because the supernatural realms are more prominent then, and using dark conjure while the realms of the supernatural are more accessible is a plus but more about this type of work later.

I'm going to offer a few guidelines for you on how to set up your altar, how to clean it and what objects to put on it to connect with and enhance your personal conjure. Remember, these are guidelines and you can follow your own intuition in the creation process to make altar workings your own. There are several books on the market that give detailed instruction on traditional placements of altar tools in hoodoo and other folk magic traditions. Here I want to give you a simple routine to work with and get you comfortable in an altar type practice. As you become more skilled in this work, you can add heavy duty traditional altar rituals to your daily routine and access its power to its full potential. Don't get too caught up in the extravagance of altar work just yet. Start small and work your way up.

You will be able to handle the conjure power of this work better that way, by progressing in small baby steps. If all you have at the time are small tea-light candles and some incense placed on your nightstand that will work to. Up in the Ozark Mountains you would not find altars specifically.

Hillbilly conjurers would have workspaces set up by the fireplace, next to a potbelly stove or in the kitchen. Folk magic was a way of life, and a granny witch or a power doctor would mix their herbs for a spell while at the same time frying up some bacon. There were no spiritual supply shops in those days in the mountains. Folks handmade their candles, used oil lamps, grew their own herbs and harvested from the hills and used what they had. If you were to walk into someone's home back in the day, and in some cases you can still find this tradition, a family would have a table set up with a bible, an oil lamp or candle and pictures of their dead family members. That was their altar, and it would not be too noticeable to those unaware that it was a conjurer's workspace. Magical herbs and such were stored with everyday kitchen utensils, and none were the wiser. Folks in the Ozarks keep their secrets, and they like it that way.

Christian Folk Magic does not have to be expensive and lavish and the traditional lore of conjure shows us that. Now on to the subject of how many altars one should have. Many practitioners have personal altars for various purposes, in addition to working altars if they provide rootworking services. Different altars may include love altars, money altars and altars for good luck and blessings. I have consolidated the number I try to work with four main altars, plus a working altar. Remember I'm offering only guidelines here, so use what works for you. These altars are for the Ancestors, Good Luck, Justice and Blessing. My main working includes my Bible, my La Madama statue and other curios. I work with La Madama most often for my own personal workings and for my clients.

Ancestor Altar

But I will remember for them the covenant with their ancestors. -

Leviticus 26:45

This altar is specific to devotions, dedications and prayers to your familial spirits.

This altar can hold pictures, belongings and offerings to the dead, along with standard vigil candles as well. If you don't feel you know any loved ones in spirit you can connect to, remember, you don't have to know all of your ancestors for them to help you. There is a long line of ancestral guardians that will come forth because you're their kith and kin. And remember you may also have ancestral spirits that will adopt you as their own, like that of the spirit of La Madama and Black Hawk.

A simple ancestor altar may include:

-White vigil candle for spiritual purity

- Offering bowl with sage and tobacco herbs for spiritual contact (You can add your ancestor's graveyard dirt)

-Glass of cool water; a traditional ancestral offering

-White altar cloth with family bible or family photo album

-Fresh flowers (Any Sort)

-Ancestor photos or belongings

Blessing Altar

The LORD bless thee, and keep thee. - Numbers 6:24-26

Your devotions and workings for matters of health, spiritual cleansings and spiritual growth are dedicated here. Images of healing saints such as Mother Mary, Jesus and Saint Jude can be placed here to bless your home and my family with their immaculate power.

A simple blessing altar may include

-Blue vigil candle for peace dressed with blessing oil

-White altar cloth & a Bible

-Images of you and your house mates/pets/family (living)

- Statue/framed images of Jesus or Mother Mary

- Fresh herbal offerings of Lavender flowers, Echinacea flowers and Bayberry which are blessing & healing herbs

- Offering bowl of redbrick dust and salt to protect the home

Good Luck Altar

He holds success in store for the upright - Proverbs 2:7

Everyone wants to create Good Luck in their life. Good Luck is an energy that we are able to invoke manifest and magnify. This altar can be dedicated to prayers and working for lady luck to enhance your money, love life and careers success. Saint Expedite is a popular guardian for this altar, the faster the luck is brought forth the better.

This simple good luck altar may include:

-Green candle vigil for money drawing or a yellow candle vigil for success dressed with Van Van Oil for drawing luck, and clearing away evil

-Green or gold altar cloth patterned with four leaf clovers or horseshoes, both good luck symbols

-An offering bowl with cinnamon sticks, allspice berries and sassafras chips soaked in Hoyts Cologne to draw in luck and good fortune.

-Statue of Saint Expedite for fast luck and a Bible

Justice Altar

When justice is done, it brings joy to the righteous but terror to evildoers. - Proverbs 21:15

Now this is an interesting altar. This one is dedicated to prayers and workings associated with conditions such as reversing baneful conjure workings, bad luck and spiritual clearings. Archangel Michael is my guardian over this altar.

This simple justice altar may include:

- White vigil candle to repel negativity dressed with Olive or Hyssop Oil for blessing

- Black cloth with a cross drawn in white for supreme protection

- Offering bowl with Rue, Devils Shoestring and Angelica Root for protection and cleansing

- Chicken foot, Railroad Spike and a Bible (All for uncrossing and protection against enemies)

- Stature or framed image of Saint Michael the sword and shield of God

Creating and Cleansing Altar Space

Here are some simple tips to cleaning your altar spaces. You will see that I use vinegar as the base in every washing remedy. Vinegar has traditionally been used to ward of illness and to clear energy. Plus, it's a wonderful all-around cleansing agent. I have fashioned each tip to be associated to the specific magical nature of each altar. Cleaning your altar is also a form of ritual and devotion. Have a bucket of water ready, because you will be adding these formulas listed below to the water. Some altars like, the Justice Altar may need be to cleaned daily depending on how much intense conjure you're doing. Most of the time I give my altar space a good washing about once a month. Always dust the altar and placements regularly keeping the energy clear and refreshed.

Ancestor Alter & Blessing Altar

Clean with cap of ½ cup of white vinegar and Florida Water. Florida Water is an old time cologne used as an offering to ancestral guides and spiritual cleansing. *Don't put salt on your ancestor altar, due to its occult nature, anything supernatural good or bad cannot cross it.

Justice Altar

Clean with a few pitches of salt. ½ cup of white vinegar. Bless a few drops of Van Van Oil to clear evil.

Good Luck Altar

Clean with ½ cup of white vinegar and bless with few splashes of Hoyts cologne.

Conjure Herbs, Roots & Curios

One of my most favorite aspects of Christian Folk Magic is rootworking conjure and potion making. This is where I can truly feel the power of conjure come alive with a mixture of the appropriate herbal blends, dressed with the proper oils and prayed over by candle light, magic truly manifests.

Having a better understanding of herbal conjure and rootworking formulary you can add an incredible amount of power to your workings for your life and wellbeing. I will include here, a select listing and glossary of herbs, roots and curios and everyday kitchen items that you can use to perform all of your cleansings, blessings and protection conjurings with. Here you will find a mixture of herbal magica sourced from Ozark and Appalachian, African-American Hoodoo, Native American and European traditions

The amazing thing about herbs in your conjure work is not only their spiritual power, but there medicinal uses as well. Again, God Almighty has given us all we need right here on this planet to fulfill your conjure and heath needs. I won't go into a big spread about the medicinal uses, there are tons of good books on the market for that; I will summarize for you. The folks who lived during the bible times were very advanced in herbalism. They always had special pots and containers set aside for their herbs, tinctures and holy oils. It was a way of life back then, not unlike the Southern Heritage of our ancestors, and for us today to have an herbal pharmacy on hand and ready for the healing and Conjure workings.

For example, let's take the herb called Hyssop. It's a member of the mint family. It is one of the most powerful herbs in the Old Testament and will add great power to your own work for Conjure. Hyssop is often referred to aid in purification and cleansing.

In the days of the Black Plague it was anointed on the inside of masks to kill the deadly virus, and therefore block any inhalations of the disease. Many doctors of that time and folks collecting dead bodies had to be covered in it. Exodus 12:22 tells us, that the people used Hyssop branches to dip into jars of blood and cover their doorframes with it. This was an act of conjuring spiritual protection under God's Power. Some old conjure workers have used this verse to stop excessive bleeding. Psalm 51:7 says "cleanse me with hyssop, and I will be clean; wash me, and I will be whiter than snow"; that pretty much says it all for the use of Hyssop in your workings. It's good for not only spiritual cleanings and protection, but for un-crossing and un-jinxing.

In Genesis 30: 14-16, we are given an example of Mandrake being used and prayed over by Bible Conjure workers in the Old Testament.

Traditionally Mandrake root was used for love and money drawing conjures. A few other herbs used for baths and holy oils were, Balm, Frankincense, Myrrh, Camphor, Saffron & Cinnamon. Here are a few more samples of biblical herbs and the scriptures associated with them. I urge you to get out the old Bible and do some research on this as well.

Anise (Matthew 23:23 KJV) - for psychic awareness and warding off evil

Coriander (Exodus 16:31; Numbers 11:7) - for luck and love drawing

Cinnamon (Exodus 30:23; Revelation 18:13) - for luck and fortune

Cumin (Isaiah 28:25; Matthew 23:23) - protection from evil

Dill (Matthew 23:23) - for uncrossing and hex-breaking

Garlic (Numbers 11:5) - for protection

Mustard (Matthew 13:31) - for faith and healing

Rue (Luke 11:42) - the amazing rue is for protection and prosperity

Holy Ghost Hoodoo Herb Magic: Waking up the Roots

First and foremost your herbs and roots are intelligent. They are alive with energy; each with their own specific spiritual empowerment for specific workings. Southern conjure workers have been working with roots and herbs for hundreds of years. God did not leave us on this earth without an herbal remedy for every single aliment, and that goes for medicinal as well as spiritual. We must respect God's holy power held within every seed, leaf and twig. There is an actual system of thought used folk magic called the Doctrine of Signatures. This belief states that the Creator marked every living herb and root with a divine signature to indicate its intended use. Every root and herb has a spirit and a purpose. This system of thought can be adapted to conjure curios as well, such as using black hen feathers to fan away and clear negativity. Chickens are always scratching and clearing away debris to catch the worm, which is reflected in the use of hen feathers for clearing. Black hen or black rooster feathers are thought to be more powerful because the color black absorbs bad luck and evil.

I have memories of my grandma letting a black hen loose in the house, letting it run here and there, then eventually out the back door. It would shake its feathers as if it were throwing something off. When I asked grandma about the odd ritual, she said it was to clear the devil out.

Your conjure work should always be handled with care and thoughtfulness. Remember, the roots will work with you, but use and abuse them, they have the "know how" to work against you. In this day and age it may be hard for a practitioner to grow and harvest their own herbs. If you can, that's the best way to go.

Herbs and roots are like extra hands and fingers to help us amplify that inner power and express it our into the universe. Having a one on one relationship with your herbs and roots from start to finish will only empower your work even more. For a lot of you that are living in the urban jungles of concrete and steel you may have to locate an herbal provider such as a local spiritual supply store, botanica or shop the internet.

Your local health food store may have many bulk herbs available, but the specific occult roots and herbs, like High John the Conquer, Queen Elizabeth Root and Devils Shoestring may have you looking for a specialty store. With the abundance of networking within the conjure community it's a snap to find retailers and even friends who can scout around for your supply needs. The most important thing to remember when buying from a secondary source is that fact that you may not know exactly where or how your herbs were picked, harvested or in some cases blessed. When your buy your herbal materials, even if they are advertised as organic, "blessed and fixed"……FIX them yourself. To "fix" means to bless them accordingly by your own will. If you trust your provider, then you have nothing to worry about as far as energy residual that may not be something you want in your conjure work. If you get herbs and roots and even oils from a company or person you do not know, bless then and wake them up on your own magical steam. Roots and herbs that have been sitting around in stock rooms or retail shops have a tendency to fall asleep. They exist in a type of dormant state till the worker wakes them up, and that happens via a blessing and incantation.

A friend of mine always prays over her meals when she eats out, not as a religious need, but as a spiritual need to cleanse the food she is about to eat. "I never know what mood the chef might be in, or the even waiter serving it to me." These are wise words that also go along with root working; remember to bless everything. If you are lucky enough to grow and harvest your own herbs for root working you will be praying over them and blessing them all the time, and that naturally plays into the conjure work you have waiting for them. The informative spiritual uses of these herbs included here were handed down from dedicated and experienced southern rootworkers and folk magic practitioners, and from my own personal practice. With hundreds of years of trial and error, they passed on, in most cases by word of mouth, an incredible catalog of information for the authentic conjure worker of today. Remember there is a spirit in every root and herb you work with. Connect to it and have a relationship with its spiritual intelligence. Respect the root, and it will stand by your side with every working.

There is blessed power over every leaf, tree, root and flower and we can access that power through Christian Folk Magic. Listed below are just a mere sample of conjure herbs, flowers and roots used for love, luck, money, blessing and protection. Many of these come from my old mountain magic backgrounds as well as the American Indian and African American folklore traditions. There are a few herbal workings listed that I have adapted for own practice as well. *To wake up the spirit within your herbs, roots and curios hold them in your hands and simply ask that the Holy Ghost to awaken its power. *Come Holy Ghost. Awaken and be Powerful in Jesus' Name!*

Angelica or the Holy Ghost Root

This is one of my most favorite roots to work with. Since I do a lot of spiritual cleansing and healing work, this root goes in the pot quite often. Angelica root is used to enhance a sense of peace and safety. It can be used in conjure workings to ward off evil and enhance spiritual protection. As powerful healing root it can be a great addition to workings for emotional balance and wellbeing.

Allspice

Allspice has long been used for money drawing conjure. It's a great herbal addition to house blessings and conjure workings for a steady stream of income.

Bayberry

I love to have this herb either fixed in a candle or mixed in an offering bowl on my good luck altar. Bayberry is a superstar her for money drawing, good fortune and prosperity workings.

Bay Leaf

This is a powerful herb used for protection, and as well as invoking clarity and psychic visions. I call it the "herb of truth." Use a Bay leaf in your conjure to ward off the evils of delusion and see the truth in any situation. It's a great protective charm against glamour magic and it will push people to tell you the truth.

Blackberry Leaves

The conjure power of blackberry leaves are used for reversal workings and banishing evil intentions back to the sender. You have the power to deflect any negative coming from you, and this herb will help you achieve it a sturdy arm of psychic protection. Light a white seven day vigil candle.

Dress the top of the candle with a few pinches of angelica root pieces that have been soaked in olive oil. Surround the vigil with a circle of blackberry leaves. Let the candle melt completely away and allow negativity to be taken with it.

Cherokee Rose

The legend of the Cherokee Rose is a story I heard all the time growing up in Arkansas. I'm sure it's partially due to the Cherokee tribal blood that flows heavily through my ancestry. The lore tells us that during the Trail of Tears which forced Cherokee tribes from the southeast to Indian Territory in Oklahoma, children were the first to parish from hunger and the bitter elements.

Each time a mother cried for her dead child, the wise ones of the tribe would pray for a sign from the Creator to aid the mother in her time of unbearable grief. The legend goes on to say that where each place a mother's tear would drop, a white rose started growing. It was named the Cherokee Rose. You can place these roses as an offering on your ancestor altar in times of grief and sadness, asking for support from you ancestral guides.

Cinnamon

This is another popular spice for money drawing as well as love and passion spells. I add cinnamon to heat up different conjure works in a positive way.

Dandelion

Here is mountain folk magic at its finest. This is a wonderful conjure herb used for workings to make dreams come true. It enhances courage to reach for the stars and achieve your goals. It can also aid in one's spiritual growth and insight.

Devils Shoestring Root

This is my most absolute favorite conjure herb to work with. If there was a patron herb or root assigned to us, this would be mine. This heavy duty root safeguards you from any evil workings and is said to literally "trip" the devil. I use it in all of my exorcism rituals, spiritual cleansings, good luck and blessings. I add a piece of this root to almost every conjure bag I make for folks. It will help cut and clear any negative blocking your way to wellbeing and prosperity.

Dogwood Flower

The dogwood flower has been a symbol of the Christian faith in the Ozark hundreds of years. According to the lore the Dogwood tree once grew tall and strong. When it was used to make the cross, Jesus was so moved that he promised the tree that it would never again be used for such a purpose. The tree now grows short, it is said the bracts of the snowy white dogwood petals resemble the cross and bare the blood red nail marks of the crucifixion. This is very powerful conjure herb magic.

I have adapted dogwood petals for use as a symbol of the four way crossroads. I use the flower petals as offerings to open the crossroads for ritual work.

Add four dogwood petals to a bowel of fresh spring water and pray the "Our Father" or a special protection prayer of your choice. Let it sit on your blessing altar for three full days with the continued blessings of your prayer. At the end of third day, strain the water into a bottle and you have a very special holy water. Add dried dog wood flowers as an herbal infusion to enhance its power.

Dragon's Blood Resin

Keeps evil away and brings spiritual empowerment and protection to the user. Dragon's Blood comes from the sap of a tree, the Dragon Palm. Naturally blood-red in color, the pure resin is burned on charcoal.

Echinacea

This major blessing herb in mountain folk magic conjure. It's an all-purpose protection charm for spiritual and physical ailments. Echinacea can add power to your conjure spells.

The roots and flowers are both used in conjure bags, and burned as incense to clear and fumigate a home.

Elder Flowers

The magic of these flowers conjure a peaceful enhancement and enhances intuitive awareness. It also helps to ward of nightmares. Place elder flowers on a blessing altar in your bedroom to invoke a peaceful setting.

Goldenseal Root

A wonderful mountain magic herb. I use goldenseal in all my healing rituals and conjure bags. This nifty herb not only adds healing to ones conjure workings, it also ward of illness and disease.

Grains of Paradise

A multi-purpose curio used for protection, legal and money matters. I also use this for block busting work, as well as adding major mojo to my workings. Grains of Paradise was a favorite of Madame Marie Laveau, the Voodoo Queen of New Orleans. She used it to win court cases for her clients.

High John the Conqueror Root

A mighty conjure root, very popular in African-American folk magic to draw luck and power. It is known to vanquish all blocks and adds power and a masculine mastery to conjure workings. This root is good one for men to use in regaining personal power in a positive way.

Horehound

In the Ozarks of Arkansas almost every mom and pop shop where you will have an abundance of horehound candy. Horehound has long been used as a treatment for lung health, but in conjure magic is reported to carry the spiritual properties for physical protection. Carry this herb in a conjure bag while traveling or hiking in unknown regions to ward off physical harm from animals or strangers. Sprinkle horehound around your camp site as well to protect against mischievous critters and curios wildlife.

Hyssop

This is a powerful Biblical conjure herb for used purification. Its high vibration adds spiritual cleansing power to your workings.

Lamb's Ear

This is a "magical softener" herb used to heal and bless. Its white wooly foliage defiantly feels like a cozy lambs ear. It's conjure is great for a blessing new born babes. It's also used for healing emotional wounds and performing forgiveness rituals.

Lavender

This is the soother of all soothers in conjure and magic. Lavender is used in love spells and can even cool down a hot temper. If Cinnamon heats you up, Lavender will cool you down. Mix lavender and spring water in an offering bowl. Add a floating tea light candle to enhance love in your home and extinguish arguments in your relationships.

Lemongrass

This is one of the top power herbs in all magical workings no matter what tradition. I'm personally never without lemongrass in its many forms as dried herb, blessed oil or a dressed candle. It's conjure properties are widely known to clear away evil and draw in luck. In African-American hoodoo lemongrass is one of the major ingredients in Van Van oil, an all-purpose conjure oil. Steep lemongrass herb in a tea, strain and add it to a bucket of spring water. Use it to wash your floors and doorways to banish negativity and draw in luck and harmony.

Master Root

This is a wonderful root to conjure up the mastery of power in any situation. It is said to increase physical vitality, willpower and stamina. I like to call it the "bionic" root. I use it in conjure bags for clients that are athletes, or are very physical and outdoorsy. I also use it in conjure workings to help people deal addiction problems, as it aids in the strength of will to overcome.

Put a piece of master root to your pocket for your daily exercise. It may help you go that extra mile.

Mugwort

This conjure herb is alleged to opens up the psychic channels to the spirit world. Put mugwort herb mixed with elder flowers in a purple sachet bag and place it in your pillow case at night to enhance psychic dreams.

Peony

This is beautiful garden plant with blooming flowers said to aid one against the winds of misfortune and increase health and longevity. If you are having a run of bad luck or just feeling poorly, steep lemongrass leaves in a tea. Add it to a tub of bath water, and throw in some Peony flower petals, the color of your choice, and soak for 20 minutes and meditate on the "Our Father" prayer. You can also burn a few tea lights dressed with Van Van Oil during the ritual. Let the misfortune go down the drain when you're done. Pat dry and carry on.

Pine Needles

Pine needles are another great conjure herb for spiritual cleansing. If you don't like lemongrass, you can substitute pine needles in its place. I also like the magical idea that since pine needles are evergreens, they are great additions to money conjure to promote a steady stream of income. Take a branch of pine needles and sweep your home's front porch or stoop to clear negativity. Also add pine needles to your altar work for money drawing for that steady stream of income.

Poke Root

This magical mountain herb brings me many fond memories. Poke root grew everywhere in the hills, and my mama used to pick it's leaves and mix up a poke salad fit for a king. I like using Poke root in my personal workings for blockbusting conjure and uncrossing. If you feel there is a block in life, put dried Poke roots in an offering bowl mixed with dandelion root and place it on your good luck altar.

Offer it to Saint Expedite, and ask that he "poke" a hole in the blockages to your desires and dreams and let the walls come down. Let the fortune flow in. Poke root is not a traditional offering to Saint Expedite, but I have found that it's a great addition.

Queen Elizabeth Root

If High John the Conquer Root is good for masculine empowerment, then Queen Elizabeth Root is like its feminine power equivalent. You can use this root in rituals for compassion, intuition, truth telling and love drawing. Offer it to Saint Martha to aid you in personal power over patriarchal masculinity. Carry Queen Elizabeth Root as a talisman for intuitive awareness by adding it to a conjure bag or even wearing it as a talisman.

Rose Petals

Rose petals are pretty much a universal symbol for love and passion in any magical circle. Roses are also a wonderful offering for Mother Mary. Take a bath in rose petals and rosemary to clear away old relationship habits and draw in new love.

Rosemary

If you want to take away foggy thoughts and mental confusion, this is your conjure herb. Rosemary has long been used for clearing and protective properties. Some workers even use it to protect their spells from interference. Take a white pillar candle, and dress it with olive oil. Then roll the candle in a bed of rosemary. Light the wick and let the candle burn down releasing the rosemary magic of clarity and focus. You can also burn rosemary as an incense to spiritually fumigate your space adding layers of protection from confusing thoughts and habits.

Rue

What would a power doctor do without Rue magic, the queen of herbs? Traditional Hoodoo folklore states that Rue has long been used for uncrossing, enhancing prosperity and aiding in exorcisms. Rue adapts very well mountain conjure. It aids and protects; adds power to conjure workings along with deflecting the evil eye. To make your own rue annotating oil, take a mason quart jar and fill it with rue leaves and flowers.

Then add olive or almond oil. Some folks even use plan vegetable oil. Fill the jar to the rim. Shake well and let stand in a dark cupboard for about 30 days; a moon cycle. Give the jar a shake now and then magnifying its blessing power. At the end of the 30 days, strain the oil. Now you have rue oil to use for dressing candles, or yourself.

Sassafras

This is not only a famous money drawing herb, it's also great for conjure working for fast luck! I often add sassafras root to offering bowls or conjure bags dedicated to speeding up a financial process to bring in material gain, ASAP. You can also use it to hurry along money that is owed to you. For a fast luck talisman, use a sachet bag of green or yellow flannel. Add a few chips of sassafras, pyrite bits and a buckeye nut. Sew the bag shut and dress it with Hoyts cologne for added good luck power. Carry on your person and let the fast track of lady luck spin you in the right direction.

Slippery Elm

In Hoodoo, this bark is used in magical workings against gossip and slander. I have also tested its spiritual properties in workings that seem to need their grinders greased to great success. If you find that a conjure working you are performing is having trouble getting off the ground add some slippery elm bits to the mix, and watch the magic smooth out. It's little like adding lotion to your conjure to create smooth results. Believe it or not, I add slippery elm to old fashioned hot foot powder recipes to banish nasty folks out of my life. I always want to make this type of conjure working a smooth one with no drama.

Tobacco

I love tobacco! It's conjure properties are used for connecting to American Indian an Ancestral spirit guides. It's a sacred herb to native tribes or opening up to the spiritual realms and connects to its wisdom. I use tobacco infused oil, plus burning it as a smoke offering to my great-grandfather.

I also use it to connect to the great Black Hawk for spiritual devotion and wisdom.

Add a few pinches of dried tobacco to a bundle of rosemary and lemongrass and burn on a charcoal disc. This will help to increase your connection to spirit, allowing only helpful guides to come to your aid.

Yarrow

Yarrow is used in conjure to enhance feelings of courage and intuition. I often tell newbies just learning folk magic to start working with Yarrow in the conjure, to help manifest self-esteem in what they do. Keep a sprig of Yarrow close by when working on a project it will help create a magical atmosphere where it is safe to have pride in what you do. It will also aid in straighten your intuition and insight to draw success.

Conjure Curios

Below you will find what I like to call Conjure odds and ends to help you achieve even further success in magical workings. There is no real category to put this, so I call them my conjure curios. The normal uses for some of these items are far less as exciting as their use in conjure. You can locate many of these folk magic tools at your local grocery, drug store and antique shop for little of nothing money wise. Also if you have a local botanic/occult shop, be their best friend. I'm all about simplifying your conjure. By now you should know that Christian Folk Magi can be accessible to anyone living in the country as well as in the city. Remember these are tools that you can use, or omit all together if they don't suit you. I have used many of the items listed, and even tried some new ones and have had great success in adapting them to Holy Ghost Hoodoo style of conjure.

Ammonia

Used in conjure as a powerful cleanser; to spiritually purify, wash away and remove crossed conditions, jinxes and all forms of evil. It is also used as a general cleansing of spiritual energy for altar spaces, homes and businesses.

Apache Tears

Roots and herbs were always my passion. But, there is one stone that I have been happy to work with over the years, and that is the apache tear. The apache tear is a type of obsidian like, volcanic glass. Indian lore states that the tears of the lovers of perished warriors, fell to the ground and turned to stone, the apache tears. My mother used to have bowels of these little darlin's sitting around, as décor but I know now they were working some magic.

Apache tear has the conjure power to bring courage to a person, as well emotional endurance during hard times. It's a strong stone, and if you need that one extra step in any situation to win the race, this is your stone.

The legend these stone also says that tears of the ancients have already been shed and carrying this stone will help you suffer no more. I often use these healing stones to conjure up a remedy for folks dealing with loss in relationship, or death.

I have found that an apache tear loves to be soaked and fed with Hoyts Cologne (Good Luck) and placed on any altar you choose. You can carry on your person in a pocket or conjure bag.

Black Cat Bone

A black cat bone is a powerful lucky charm used in the African American magical tradition of hoodoo. I have adopted this curio into my own practice. It is thought to ensure good luck and protection from dark magic.

Black Cat Oil

Authentic black cat bones are preserved in this master hoodoo oil from which the Lucky Black Cat Oil is made. This is a traditional hoodoo formula for luck and money used to break bad luck spells and hexes. Anoint lucky dice or a favorite lucky rabbit's foot.

Can be used as a dressing oil for candles or for feeding a gamblers conjure bag. Other ingredients include sage, bay laurel, grains of paradise, iron, lodestone and black cat hair.

Black Coffee

Used in traditional conjure to strip energy away. Also used as an offering to ancestral spirits.

Black Hen/Rooster Feathers

I do love to use black hen or black rooster feathers when I'm cleansing my home or a client. Chicken hens, especially black hens have always been look upon as a fowl of protection in the south. Their ability to scratch away dirt and debris to get their meal was looked on by hill folks as a powerful symbol of clearing and cleansing. The color black of course is the color that absorbs negativity. There black feathers have been used in brooms, and hand sweeps to sweep out evil and curses. You can find black hen feathers very easily by visiting a local farm or a neighbor with chickens and gather loose feathers with no harm to our fine feathered friends.

Some spiritual supply stores sell "ready-made" black hen feathers sweeps for purchase.

Broom Straws

For conjurers and power doctors alike, having one or more brooms is essential to a magical practice. Brooms sweep away negative energy, and can also sweep in luck and good fortune. Brooms straws can be used in conjure bags for cleaning and protection rituals as well as in baths to wash away energetic debris.

Broom Straw Oil Recipe

Take three broom straws (broom corn), cut to a ½ inch or so in length and soak them in holy water for three days; symbolizing the Holy Trinity. For each of the three days, keep the soaking straws on your blessing altar, pray over them with Psalm 23 (The Lord is My Shepard) before sunrise.

On the third day add the straws to a either a 2 ounce or 4 ounce glass bottle. Use almond oil or olive oil as a carrier with a drop or two of Vitamin E oil to help preserve its shelf life. Add a few pinches of dried Rue herb for added protection.

Shake to activate and use to anoint your ritual cleansing brooms, alter tools and even yourself. As an additional bonus, you can add a few drops of orange essential oil to your mixture as well to enhance wellbeing while cleansing.

Buckeye Nuts

Long used in the Ozarks as a good luck charm for money and prosperity.

Camphor Resin (Natural)

Extremely powerful exorcism and spiritual cleaning agent. Place a block of camphor in a bowl of water and keep it underneath your bed to spiritually cleanse your home. You may also grate the camphor block and burn it on top of charcoal for house blessings.

Chalk

Chalk is traditionally used in Christian folk magic to draw marks or sigils on altars, walk ways or doorways for blessing.

Chicken Feet (Dried)

Dried chicken feet are an essential tool for Christian folk magic practitioners. Traditionally used for spiritual cleansing and the "scratching" away of bad luck and ill-will. Carry for protection and extra power.

Chinese Floor Wash

Chinese Floor Wash is an old hoodoo formula that removes remove bad luck and restores good vibes. Its scent is similar to that of Van Van oil and Hindu Grass formulas.

Chinese Wash recipe:

- 6 oz unscented liquid castile soap
- 3 oz Murphy's oil soap
- 6 oz distilled water
- 1/2 tsp citronella oil
- 1/2 tsp lemongrass oil
- 3 pieces broom straw
- A few pinches of dried lemongrass
- a 16 oz bottle for storage

Conjure/Blessing Bags

Conjure bags go by many names like medicine bag, mojo bag, or blessing bag. In the hoodoo tradition conjure bags are made of flannel cloth or leather and tied with a drawstring. Inside, you will find most likely magic charms, herb and animal curios and written prayers which have been prayed over, to accomplish a type of magical spell like good luck drawing or spiritual protection. For a love drawing conjure bag, take a red or pink flannel cloth bag add dried rose petals, lavender and a whole John the Conquer Root for a male or whole Queen Elizabeth Root for a female depending on the sex of the person you want to draw into your life. Anoint the bag with Hoyts Cologne to draw good luck in your love life. Add this written spell to the bag, and allow the love conjure to awaken.

I draw to me a love most cherished, a love that will never parish. By herb and root I cast this spell for a partner's love that will never fail. By the Power of Three, The Holy Trinity, I conjure thee.

Corn Meal

I always wondered why my grandma kept little sachets of cornmeal at every corner of the house. Cornmeal is a wonderful agent for blessing in conjure. My grandmother's Cherokee blood held an ancient belief in the sacredness and blessing power of cornmeal. Corn was a special gift to native peoples from the Creator.

I find it especially comforting that the Cherokee held a high respect for their very own corn goddess deity, Selu the Corn Mother. You can keep an offering bowl of corn meal on your ancestor altar, and even use it to purify your blessing altar by sprinkling some around its perimeters.

Corn Soap

Grandpa's brand of Indian corn soap is an incredible spiritual blessing soap. Can be used to cleans and honor Native American spirit guides or ancestors during a ritual bath.

Dirt Dauber Nest

Used in all domination work but it is also good in enemy work. It adds extra power and a "sting" to justice work.

Florida Water

This vintage cologne is used for spiritual purification, and cleansing. Florida Water is commercially prepared toilet water that blends an array of floral essential oils in a water-alcohol base. It's been around since the early 1800's. The name refers to the fabled Fountain of Youth said to have been located somewhere in Florida. No one really knows how Florida Water came to be used in conjure and spiritual service work, but time has proven the spirits of conjure love it. I use it for a daily refresher of my energy, and cleanse my ritual tools and altars with it.

Spiritual Use Florida Water Cologne

- Floorwash– Add Florida Water to your normal cleaning mixtures to add blessings of protection.
- Remove Negativity Bath – Draw a bath, add a few splashes of Florida Water and ½ cup of sea salt.

- Laundry Rinse – Add a dash of Florida Water to your final laundry rinse to bless and protect your clothes.
- Use it as Offering Water in the cemetery to honor the ancestors.
- Use it as Offering Water at the Crossroads to open your path.
- Sprinkle on windowsills and thresholds to protect your home and welcome good energy.

Gun Powder

Used to heat up conjure workings for quick activation; an explosion of power. Also used in blockbuster work.

Hen Eggs

Eggs have always been a universal symbol of healing and well-being. It's not surprising that one of the many mountain folk healing remedies for spiritual healing is egg cleansing. Eggs are believed to absorb negativity and break curses. Take your hen egg at room temperature and bathe it in holy water or Florida Water. Let it dry. Write your name on the egg three times. Careful not to break it.

Take the egg and start at the top of your head and move the egg down in front of you, praying the "our father" and then keep moving the egg all the way down to your feet.

Start again on the left side moving the egg down from the top of the head to the feet. Still praying. Repeat on your right side from the top down. Have a friend move the egg from the back of your head down your back to the feet. When the cleansing ritual is over, take the egg, and as some traditionalists do, break it against a tree, or toss it in running water breaking the curse or letting the negative flow away from you. .

Hoyts Cologne

Here is wonderful old time cologne that has been around for years, and has mysteriously become a spiritual cologne for spell work. My grandfather used this stuff all the time. I only I wish I knew way back when to grab some of his old Hoyts' bottles. Hoyts Cologne is said to be used by gamblers for luck. Old timey root workers also use it feed conjure and mojo bags to keep them powerful. I use this stuff to empower my work.

I slap some on myself in the mornings before my prayers and it gives me an extra boost in my invocations to the Almighty. It's great to anoint your herbs, and altar statues with, as well as adding power and luck to anything you are doing. Hoyts has a strong floral scent, with a subtleness of clove and citrus. *Add devils shoestring root to a bottle of Hoyt's for an amplified effect of luck and success.

Lightning Struck Wood

Adds power and protection to any work. Use as an offering to Father Black Hawk.

Loadstones

Lodestones are naturally magnetized magnetic iron ore. They are prized in folk-magic for their "drawing" power of luck, love, protection and prosperity.

Murphy's Oil Soap

This old school household cleanser contains citronella oil; used for attracting good luck. Murphy's Oil Soap is an affordable and effective tool for when you need to do a thorough cleansing where washing the floors, wiping down walls, baseboards, window sills and door-frames, as well as other surfaces.

Offering Bowl

An offering bowl can be placed on each of your altars, filled with the appropriate herbs, oils and curios. The helpful spirits love offering bowls and it's a wonderful way to connect with the Creative Forces an open the way for conjure to fill your life. An offering bowl can be made of ceramic, clay, glass or wood. I personally don't care for plastics.

Oil Lamps

One of the oldest tools used in Christian folk magic. Oil lamps can be burned for used for love, money, protection and domination. Herbs, roots and other curios can be added to the oil lamp base for specific workings.

Pennies and Dimes

Used as payment or offerings to Ancestors and Crossroads Spirits. Hillfolks often leave a few pennies or dimes at the entrance of cemeteries as a respect to the spirits there, plus a payment to the guardian of the graves for a peaceful entrance. You can also as mentioned in an earlier chapter open the crossroads by throwing a few dimes and pennies into its center and invoking the crossroads spirit make the way between you and the supernatural accessible.

Pine Sol (Original)

Original Pine Sol is also an affordable and excellent spiritual cleanser as it contains pine oil (make sure you get the "original" pine Sol. It has actual pine oil as an ingredient). Pine is not only a strong cleanser, but it can draw steady money through its properties as an evergreen.

Pyrite

For drawing good fortune, money and successful business workings. These little bits of "fool's gold" are actually one of a conjurer's best tools and ingredients, no fooling.

You can add bits of pyrite to anything like an oil or herb mixture to enhance drawing power to your conjure.

Raccoon Penis Bone

Raccoon penis bones "lucky pecker bones" are commonly used in the Ozark Mountains as charms and curios to bring love, fertility, and luck in gambling. Add to a mojo bag with a $5.00 bill for amazing luck in gambling. Tie a red string around it and give to the object of your affection to make them fall in love with you.

Railroad Spikes

This very strong curio is used in conjure to "nail down" your enemies, protect your home and property and bring more power to your folk magic workings. Drive railroad spikes into the ground on the corners of your property to insure protection. As you drive the railroad spikes into the ground with a hammer, recite Psalms 1:3 *And he shall be like a tree planted by the rivers of water, that bringeth forth his fruit in his season; his leaf also shall not wither; and whatsoever he doeth shall prosper.*

Red Brick Dust

Old style hoodoo conjure used for the protection. Sprinkle across doorways and around the yard for blessing and keeping enemies out. If you live in an apartment, are do not have a yard just add a little offering bowl of brick dust to your blessing altar, or justice altar asking that it's power surround your home and family at all times.

Salt

Every grain offering of yours, moreover, you shall season with salt, so that the salt of the covenant of your God shall not be lacking from your grain offering; with all your offerings you shall offer salt. - Leviticus 2:13

Biblical power house of spiritual blessing and cleansing. The Convenate of Salt guarantees our blessings, preservation and protection under God.

Skeleton Key

Used for a variety of conjure working. An iron skeleton key can be used as a pendulum for opening all doors to insights in divination.

Also used for crossroads conjure workings opens all doors and roadways. Keep a pair of skeleton keys on your good luck chosen altar. Keep them in a cross form + to keep all doors open to blessings and good luck. You can also use the pair to close the doors and banish bad fortune, slander and negativity by placing them in a form of an **X** on your justice altar. Saint Peter is also petitioned using skeleton keys; he holds the "keys" to the Kingdom of God.

Van Van Oil

Louisiana Van Van is the most popular and cherished of all classic Hoodoo formulas. An all-purpose blend used for clearing evil, luck drawing and blessing. Use to anoint the body, dress candles, talismans, and feed and nurture mojo bags. Van van is derived from the french-Louisiana pronunciation of vervain as "vaah vahn". It is traditionally created from 5 oriental plants; citronella, vervain, lemongrass, galangal, and patchouli. All Van Van should contain lemongrass, some contain ginger or gingergrass.

White Vinegar

I use white or clear vinegar for permanently removing energy. Vinegar is like salt in the fact it strips down energy and defuses it. Use it in spiritual washes when cleaning household floors, window sills and altar rooms.

Dirts

Dirt's are used to draw grounding, power and intention to conjure working in a variety of ways. The magical properties of dirt, depending on its location, can be used for ancestor reverence, spirit contact as well as justice workings.

- Bank Dirt: Used for money works and financial security.
- Court House Dirt: Used for Justice and court case work
- Police Station Dirt: Used for protection work and can also be used to draw or repel the law.
- Church Dirt: Used for blessings, healings and protection work.
- Hospital Dirt: Used for all healing works.

- Forrest Dirt: Library- Used for wisdom, knowledge, research, and quietness
- Crossroads Dirt: Used for opening or closing roads in Conjure Work.
- Graveyard Dirt: Used for a variety of conjure works; blessing, protection or justice.
- Marketplace Dirt: Used for money drawing, employment, and business success.

Waters

Fresh Waters: well water, spring water, rain water, and creek water are all used to refresh the spirit of one's work.

- Storm Water: Used to stir things up in Conjure workings
- Ditch Water/Stagnate Water: Used for bindings, confusion, crossing and enemy work.
- Stump Water: Used for all varieties of healing work
- Dish Water: Used for cleansing and releasing work.
- River Water: Used for removal work.

- Lightening Water: Used for heating ones conjure up; activating power.
- Tar Water: Used for protection and uncrossing as well as the reversed.

Conjure Workings & Formulas

Bullet Protection Talisman

Take an empty rifle shell and clean it with salt, or Florida Water. Add a piece of Devils Shoestring root in the casing. Pray the "Our Father" over it and seal it with black candle wax. *Some folk add dirt from an ancestor's grave in the casing as well.

Catch a Thief

This is an old hoodoo divination method using the Holy Bible and a skeleton key. Tie the skeleton, blessed with Florida Water, to a red or white string. It should hang like a pendulum. Open your Bible to Psalm 115:1 *"Not unto us, O LORD, not unto us, but unto thy name give glory, for thy mercy, and for thy truth's sake."* Hold the skeleton key in you right hand and let it dangle over Psalm 115:1 and vocalize the scripture three times.

Then call out the name of the person you suspect has stolen from you. Pay attention to the direction the key begins moving. If it's standing still the said person is not involved. If it circles in a counter clockwise motion, they are guilty.

Mason Jar Spell to Ward off Evil

Combine a teaspoon of grains of paradise, three devils shoestring roots, a holy card of Saint Michael and ½ a cup of blessed salt in a pint size mason jar. Place it behind the front door and shake it every day to keep evil away. You can also perform this when you are gone to safeguard your home.

Hyssop and Rue Spiritual Cleansing Bath

Boil and handful of hyssop and rue in a gallon of water. Allow to cool and then strain. Add this herbal infusion to your bath water and soak for 20 mins, head to toe. While soaking recite Psalm 51:7 three times. Pat dry.

Hoyt's Hand Wash

Fill a bottle with a pump with a pure castile soap, add some Hoyts cologne and now you some powerful lucky hand wash. Add a lodestone or piece of pyrite for extra mojo.

To Stop Slanderous Bullies

"For they intended evil against thee: they imagined a mischievous device, which they are not able to perform."

Psalm 21:11 is prayer to cast against anyone being slanderous towards you. Dress a white 7 day vigil candle with Van Van Oil. Light it, and let it burn the full five to seven days and recite the prayer every morning before dawn. This will help put a stop to your bullies. The white candle stands for the purity of truth. Van Van Oil is an all-purpose conjure oil that clears the way, repels evil and reinstates good luck.

Charms against Haints and Haunts

- Tie a cross onto an iron railroad spike and place in the front window or the front door to keep out haints and haunts.

- Pour salt across doorways and windowsills to repel ghosts from entering your home.
- Splash some Florida Water on whenever you feel like you have been affected with the presence of negative spirits.
- Burn dragons blood resin and camphor to repel evil spirits.
- Tie three devils shoestrings roots together with a red string. Hang over your front door for supernatural protection.

Easy Good Luck Bath

- Handful of lemongrass
- Handful of Rue

Simmer the herbs in a gallon of spring water for 3 minutes, then strain and allow to cool. Add to morning bathwater, with a few splashes of Florida Water before heading out for the day.

Coffee Bath

Add a pot of strong black coffee to your bathwater for spiritual cleansing and wellbeing. Bathe for 20 minutes. Recite the Lord's Prayer.

Hoodoo, Conjure and Folk Magic Definitions

Bad Thing: Refers to witchcraft performed as a way of hurting, killing, or poisoning someone.

Black Magic: The work of witches that has been empowered by the Devil or by evil spirits.

Charm: Refers to conjure used to protect, heal, or drive out evil spirits. Can either refer to a physical object that is carried or to a verbal charm, such a silent prayer.

Church Fan/Conjure Fan: A church fan or a black hen feather fan can be used to sweep the body using blessed incense to uncross and exorcise an individual in Jesus' name.

Clairvoyance: (clear seeing or second sight) is a spiritual gift of the Holy Ghost where psychic impressions are spiritually or mentally perceived.

Conjure: To "summon up" using the supernatural power of the Holy Ghost.

Crossing and Uncrossing: Crossing refers to folk magic that cause harm or bad luck, while uncrossing refers to folk magic that reverse it.

Drawing: Usually refers to attracting divine favor, luck, love or fortune.

Faith Healing: Spiritual healing via the Holy Ghost using verbal prayers, laying on of hands and charms.

Folk Magic: is a term that is used to describe a set of magical practices that is usually practiced by "common folk" or country dwellers.

Foot Track Magic: Foot track magic involves throwing sachet powders in the path of a targeted person. That individual will suffer from unusual problems and a streak of bad luck after they have walked on it. The belief is that the "hexed" ingredients of the powder will be absorbed through the foot and "curse" the individual.

Floor Washes: Floor washes are used to remove negativity from the home or business or to bring good fortune, increase the number of customers, or attract love.

Florida Water is commonly used as a floor wash. A ritual floor washing typically starts at the back of the premises and ends at the front doorstep.

Ghosts, Spirits, and Haints: Restless spirits of the dead; lost souls roaming the earth.

Gift: Refers to "clairvoyant sight" a natural ability given by God.

Goomer Doctor: Similar concept to the witch doctor, someone who uses charms and prayers in as a way to remove "goomering" or witchcraft. This form of folk magician is accepted by most Ozark hillfolk as a servant of God.

Granny Witch: In this case witch is used in a positive sense and refers to a healer. Name given to older women who act as healers and midwives. Often heard in the Ozarks. Most likely comes from the Appalachian Mountains.

Hoodoo: (African American Folk Magic): Also called conjure and rootwork; refers to the practice of Southern American folk magic mostly steeped in New Orleans and the Mississippi Delta.

Hot Footing: A type of conjure ritual intended to drive a person, such as an enemy or some other troublesome person, away. Hot Foot powder is a traditional hoodoo preparation intended to rid you of unwanted people.

There are many variations on the Hot Foot powder recipe, though they almost always contain cayenne pepper. It is a mixture of powder, herbs and minerals and usually other ingredients such as sulfur, black pepper, graveyard dirt, bluestone, gunpowder, and all manner of fiery ingredients.

Mediumship: is a form of divination in which the medium communicates messages from spirits, most often the spirits of the dead. Ancestor communication.

Power Doctor: The Power Doctor is someone who heals using the power of verbal charms, Bible verses, and certain rituals.

Reader: A Root-worker, or spiritual practitioner, who is psychically gifted.

Root-worker: A practitioner of Hoodoo and Christian Folk Magic.

Setting Lights: A term which refers to the process of preparing a candle for an individual's petition and praying over it daily until it has burned out.

Spell, spellwork: Usually used in a negative sense referring to practitioners of the dark arts.

Spiritual Baths: Spiritual bathing is an ancient practice. In hoodoo, spiritual baths are taken to cleanse oneself of negativity or to bring good luck. This is often done in conjunction with the recitation of special psalms. Removing negativity requires washing oneself with a downward stroke, while bringing luck or fortune requires washing oneself in an upward motion.

A simple but powerful spiritual path remedy consists of filling a tub up with water; add a ½ cup of sea salt and a few splashes of Florida Water. Soak for 20 minutes from head to toe. Recite the "Our Father". Pat dry.

Closing Remarks

The Lord shall command the blessing upon you in your storehouse and in all that you undertake. And He will bless you in the land which the Lord your God gives you. ...And the Lord shall make you have a surplus of prosperity, through the fruit of your body, of your livestock, and of your ground, in the land which the Lord swore to your fathers to give you.- Deuteronomy 28:8, 11

As I come to the close of this particular work on the Holy Ghost Hoodoo it is my hope and prayer that you receive blessings and abundance from its pages. There is a magical world out there, and most importantly there is a magical world within you. By realizing your innate power of Conjure through Christian Folk Magic you can choose never to be fearful again when it comes to your security and safety in this life. God Almighty has planted the seed of Victory within your Soul, and through awakening the Power of Conjure, you can make that successful seed grow and prosper in everything you do. God Bless! – Rev. Darrin

BIO

Rev. Darrin W. Owens is a leading psychic expert in the metaphysical and paranormal fields. His current work focuses on psychic development, clairvoyant healing and spiritual growth. Darrin has worked full-time in the field since 1995. His openness to Spirit and his energetic teaching style gives a refreshing new look at age old metaphysical concepts of the Bible dealing with spiritual healing, the paranormal and spirit-filled living.

www.psychicdarrinowens.com

Printed in Great Britain
by Amazon